FAITH

Hymns to the

CREATOR

GAIL RAMSHAW

Augsburg Fortress
PUBLISHERS

SING THE FAITH

Hymns to the

CREATOR

GAIL RAMSHAW

Editors:
Gloria E. Bengtson,
Jeffrey S. Nelson, and
Sarah Anondson
Cover design:
Marti Naughton

Scripture quotations
are from New Revised
Standard Version
Bible, copyright
© 1989 Division of
Christian Education
of the National
Council of the
Churches of Christ in
the United States of
America. Used by
permission.

INTRODUCTION

Welcome to Sing the Faith!

Welcome to *Hymns to the Creator,* one of nine volumes in the Sing the Faith Bible study series. You are embarking on a biblical exploration of grace through the poetry, music, and history of five of the most beloved hymns of the Christian tradition.

Hymns are the faith people sing. The lyrics are owned by the people as the fabric of their theology. Many hymns have been in the memories of churchgoers for years. The melodies and texts of hymns are often retained after most other memory has faded. This series will allow participants to connect these well-loved hymns to biblical texts.

Pastors and worship leaders spend a significant amount of time searching for hymns related to the Sunday readings, the theme, and the mood of each service. Indexes are available to assist planners in coordinating biblical texts and songs. The Sing the Faith series brings this information and its powerful faith formation capability to you.

Each session focuses on one hymn. Participants will reflect on their personal history with the hymn, explore biblical connections in the texts, learn the history and legends associated with the hymn, and consider how the message of the hymn applies to their daily journey of faith.

Preparing your study

The Sing the Faith series, designed for small-group Bible study, encourages interaction among participants to help them grow and enrich their journeys of faith. Alternate groupings, with minor modifications, would be possible. Individuals might use this resource for personal study or partner with another individual to study and correspond by phone or e-mail.

The thematically connected hymns in each volume can be studied at any time and in any church season.

The material is planned for weekly gatherings. The meeting place could be at church or in homes. The key will be finding a place where everyone can feel safe as they share, reflect, and pray together.

This study is ideal for rotational leadership. As leaders and participants discover an increased connection between worship and study, their understanding of leadership will continue to broaden. If a pastor is a part of your group, include him or her in the rotation. The opportunity to operate as a participant will be welcomed.

Adults of all ages and stages will find this study useful—singles groups, men's breakfasts, mom's time out, and new member study are just a few ideas. Because of the universality of the hymns used in this series, a young adult group may be as vital as an older adult group.

Planning each session

Gathering for the story

The first three pages of each session introduce the hymn. The instructions invite you to transition from a time of fellowship as you arrive, to gathering your thoughts about the hymn, checking in with each other, then experiencing the hymn (see page 6), and finally praying together.

Learning the story

This section provides relevant information about the text, the tune, and the legends of each hymn. The intent is not in-depth study, but an opportunity to discover stories and anecdotes about the persons and circumstances that were a part of the creation of the hymn.

Our story

Hymns and songs carry emotional and cognitive memories. In this section, you will be asked to reflect on how the hymn has been part of your growth in the Christian faith. The questions, similar in all sessions, provide time and a safe opportunity to share how the music and poetry has affected who we are as believers.

The biblical story

Unless the hymn writer indicated a specific biblical passage, the intended textual connection can never be certain. The writer of this study discovered textual connections and images for one stanza of each hymn and has provided questions to help you search for personal meaning related to faith traditions and the Bible.

Texts were selected from the New Revised Standard Version of the Bible (NRSV), but each participant may use his or her own Bible. Using a variety of translations can bring new perspectives to your discussions.

Additional questions to reflect on in this section of the study are:

- ◆ What is normally taken for granted about this passage?
- ◆ What is related to your own journey of faith?
- ◆ What connections to biblical and doctrinal understanding do you find?
- ◆ What may affect you personally in this text?

Living the story

Each hymn study ends with several questions addressing how this hymn will affect the way you live your faith as a result of your learning. What message will you bring to each day?

Each session ends with praying and singing. The closing prayer (with time for individual petitions) and singing the hymn weave new dimensions to the hymn's familiar words and images.

Experiencing the hymn

An important part of this study is the experience of singing. Whether your group is large or small, raise your voices together each week. If a piano and accompanist are available, look for the full score in your favorite hymnal. Most hymns are included in *Lutheran Book of Worship* or *With One Voice*, and may be found in most traditional Christian hymnals.

If your group has instrumentalists, invite them to play with you as you sing. Perhaps someone's hidden talent will shine! Invite a young person or two from your congregation who play in their school orchestra or band to play along for one session.

Many of the hymns in the Sing the Faith volumes appear on numerous recordings. The reference list on page 47 offers a starting place for your search. You might publicize your study in your church newsletter or bulletin by listing the hymns and asking for recording recommendations. In addition, piano collections that include one or more of the hymns are suggested on this page.

Whether you sing *a cappella* or with a pipe organ at its fullest, enjoy your time with the music, with the texts, with memories of the past and hope for the future, and with each other as together you Sing the Faith.

ALL CREATURES, WORSHIP GOD MOST HIGH

1 All creatures, wor - ship God most high! Sound ev - 'ry voice in
2 Sing, broth - er wind; with clouds and rain you grow the gifts of
3 O fire, our broth - er, mirth - ful, strong, drive far the shad - ows,
4 All who for love of God for - give, all who in pain or

earth and sky: Al - le - lu - ia! Al - le - lu - ia!
fruit and grain: Al - le - lu - ia! Al - le - lu - ia!
join the throng: Al - le - lu - ia! Al - le - lu - ia!
sor - row grieve: Al - le - lu - ia! Al - le - lu - ia!

Sing, broth - er sun, in splen - dor bright; sing, sis - ter moon
Dear sis - ter wa - ter, use - ful, clear, make mu - sic for
O earth, our moth - er, rich in care, praise God in col -
Christ bears your bur - dens and your fears; still make your song

Refrain

and stars of night:
your Lord to hear: Al - le - lu - ia, al - le - lu - ia,
ors bright and rare:
a - mid the tears:

al - le - lu - ia, al - le - lu - ia, al - le - lu - ia!

Text: Martin A. Seltz, based on a hymn of St. Francis of Assisi. © 1999 Augsburg Fortress. Used with permission.
Music: LASST UNS ERFREUEN, *Geistliche Kirchengesänge*, Köln, 1623.

GATHERING FOR THE STORY

Greet participants as they arrive. Invite them to record their responses to these questions in their book.

A Bible concordance would be a helpful tool for people who want to list text citations or search for stories by key words.

Begin with introductions. Ask volunteers to share the stories they selected, then say the prayer together.

Invite the group to sing "All Creaures, Worship God Most High" (see page 7). *(10 minutes)*

When do you hear birds sing? Although scientists tell us that birds sing to mark their territory, many Christian hymns say that not only are birds praising God, but that all creation praises God by being what it is. How does the earth itself praise God?

Do you like this hymn? Why or why not?

O God most high,
    we join with one another and with
    your whole creation to sing your praises.
Your sun is splendid, your moon bright,
    your fire strong.
Give us the breath to speak your story,
    the mind to study your word,
    and the will to sing your song;
through Jesus Christ,
    our Savior and Lord. Amen

ALL CREATURES, WORSHIP GOD MOST HIGH

All creatures, worship God most high!
Sound ev'ry voice in earth and sky: Alleluia! Alleluia!
Sing, brother sun, in splendor bright;
sing, sister moon and stars of night:
Alleluia, alleluia, alleluia, alleluia, alleluia!

Sing, brother wind; with clouds and rain
you grow the gifts of fruit and grain: Alleluia! Alleluia!
Dear sister water, useful, clear,
make music for your Lord to hear:
Alleluia, alleluia, alleluia, alleluia, alleluia!

O fire, our brother, mirthful, strong,
drive far the shadows, join the throng: Alleluia! Alleluia!
O earth, our mother, rich in care,
praise God in colors bright and rare:
Alleluia, alleluia, alleluia, alleluia, alleluia!

All who for love of God forgive,
all who in pain and sorrow grieve: Alleluia! Alleluia!
Christ bears your burdens and your fears;
still make your song amid the tears:
Alleluia, alleluia, alleluia, alleluia, alleluia!

Come, sister death, your song release
when you enfold our breath in peace: Alleluia! Alleluia!
Since Christ our light has pierced your gloom,
fair is the night that leads us home.
Alleluia, alleluia, alleluia, alleluia, alleluia!

O sisters, brothers, take your part,
and worship God with humble heart: Alleluia! Alleluia!
All creatures, bless the Father, Son,
and Holy Spirit, Three in One:
Alleluia, alleluia, alleluia, alleluia, alleluia!

Text: Martin A. Seltz, based on a hymn of St. Francis of Assisi.
© 1999 Augsburg Fortress. Used with permission.

LEARNING THE STORY

After participants read the hymn background, talk about information they found meaningful or helpful.

(5 minutes)

The text

Francis of Assisi (1182–1225) wrote this hymn, called the "Canticle of Brother Sun," in his Italian dialect during the last year of his life. In the early twentieth century, the Anglican clergyman William Henry Draper paraphrased the poem into stanzas for use at a children's festival. The version printed here, closer to the original than Draper's, was crafted by Martin A. Seltz (b. 1951).

The tune

LASST UNS ERFREUEN was first printed in a German Roman Catholic hymnal in 1623. The tune became popular for English-speaking Christians when it appeared in 1906 as the tune for "Ye Watchers and Ye Holy Ones." A powerful but very simple tune, the notes mostly go up and down the scale.

The legend

The beloved saint Francis saw himself as united with all of God's creation and as one with even the smallest creatures. During the last year of his life, Francis, nearly blind from an eye disease, in constant severe pain, and lying in a hut overrun with mice, wrote the joyous "Canticle of Brother Sun," in which he calls all creation his mother, his brothers, and his sisters. He sees even death as part of the beautiful natural world that God created. Francis' death is observed around the world on October 4.

OUR STORY

Do you consider the creation to be Mother Earth? In what way(s) could creation be considered Mother Earth? If you do not think of creation in this way, share your image of creation.

You may need to adapt these questions for the participants in your group. Ask them to record their responses and then share their stories.

(10 minutes)

Can you imagine a time when fire could be "mirthful"? Describe such a time.

How appropriate is it to think of death as your sister? Explain.

THE BIBLICAL STORY

Invite participants to find the passages in their Bibles and record responses to the questions.

In some religions, earth is a harmful place created by an evil deity. In the Bible, God created the world and called it very good (see Genesis 1:31). If the world is good, what is our relationship to it?

Francis's canticle is like Psalm 148, in which all creation praises God. Many Christians sing this psalm on the Sunday after Christmas. Which line in this psalm speaks to you? Why?

A Jewish legend says that when King Nebuchadnezzar threw the three young men into the fiery furnace, they sang a song entitled "All You Works of the Lord, Bless the Lord." This canticle (LBW 18) is found in many contemporary worship books, and some Christians sing it at the Easter Vigil. Describe an occasion when you might sing this canticle.

Determine if your group would prefer to:

◆ read and respond to all passages and questions before talking

◆ read, respond, and discuss one passage at a time

(20 minutes)

The Greek word alleluia *expresses the Hebrew phrase "praise the LORD!" (See Psalm 117, among others.) Would you rather sing "alleluia" or "praise the Lord"? Why?*

LIVING THE STORY

Invite participants to reflect for a few moments on today's conversation, and then respond to the questions. It is important to share the responses to these questions so your group can offer prayer support to each other throughout the week.

Select a leader for your next meeting and remind everyone of the time and location.

Close by singing "All Creatures, Worship God Most High" and praying together.
(10 minutes)

Can Christians experience this hymn? How?

What does it mean to sing God's praises? When and how does the Church do this?

What do you think about singing this hymn when facing death? How is this a hymn for hospice?

O God most high, we join once again
    with your whole creation
    to sing your praises. Your earth is a gift,
     your creation is filled with your goodness
    and light.
(Silence for private prayer).
Give us joy in your earth,
    connect us with all that you have made,
    and make us ready when death comes;
through Jesus Christ,
    our Savior and Lord. Amen

MOTHERING GOD, YOU GAVE ME BIRTH

1 Moth - er - ing God, you gave me birth
2 Moth - er - ing Christ, you took my form,
3 Moth - er - ing Spir - it, nur - t'ring one,

in the bright morn - ing of this world.
of - fer - ing me your food of light,
in arms of pa - tience hold me close,

Cre - a - tor, source of ev - 'ry breath,
grain of new life, and grape of love,
so that in faith I root and grow

you are my rain, my wind, my sun.
your ver - y bod - y for my peace.
un - til I flow'r, un - til I know.

Text: © Jean Janzen. Used by permission.
Music: NORWICH, Carolyn Jennings, b. 1936. © 1995 Augsburg Fortress.

GATHERING FOR THE STORY

The Christian creeds call God, our Creator, father. Do you ever think of the Creator as mother? Why or why not?

Greet participants as they arrive. Invite them to record their responses to these questions in their book.

A Bible concordance would be a helpful tool for people who want to list text citations or search for stories by key words.

Begin with introductions. Ask volunteers to share the stories they selected, then say the prayer together.

Invite the group to sing "Mothering God, You Gave Me Birth" (see page 15). *(10 minutes)*

What is the difference for you between the metaphors of "father" and "mother"?

O God our Creator,
    you are the source of our every breath.
    You mother us with your care,
    and you nurture our faith and life.
Be with us now as we together
    seek your face and praise your love;
    through Jesus Christ,
our Savior and Lord. Amen

MOTHERING GOD,
YOU GAVE ME BIRTH

Mothering God, you gave me birth
in the bright morning of this world.
Creator, source of ev'ry breath,
you are my rain, my wind, my sun.

Mothering Christ, you took my form,
offering me your food of light,
grain of new life, and grape of love,
your very body for my peace.

Mothering Spirit, nurt'ring one,
in arms of patience hold me close,
so that in faith I root and grow
until I flow'r, until I know.

LEARNING THE STORY

After participants read the hymn background, talk about information they found meaningful or helpful.

(5 minutes)

The text

Julian lived in Norwich, England, in the fourteenth century. She spent most of her long life as a solitary, residing in a hut attached to the village church. Through one window she attended to the church services, through a second gave pastoral counseling, and through the third communicated with her servant. After sixteen visions of Christ, she wrote about their meaning in a book entitled *Revelations of Divine Love*—the first book written by a woman in English. In 1991, Jean Janzen, a California Mennonite poet and teacher, adapted some of Julian's writings into this hymn.

The tune

Carolyn Henderson Jennings, professor of music at St. Olaf College, composed this tune for Janzen's hymn text and titled the tune NORWICH.

The legend

During the fourteenth century, life in England was exceedingly harsh. The plague killed many people, and the church was dominated by issues of sin, purgatory, and hell. Yet Julian wrote eloquently about God the mother, loving and caring for us all. Since in the fourteenth century people thought that mother's milk was made out of a woman's blood, she wrote that the blood of Holy Communion was like milk coming from Christ, her mother. The famous line, "All shall be well, and all shall be well, and all manner of things shall be well" is Julian's.

Our Story

In what ways is God, our Creator, like a mother? Explain.

You may need to adapt these questions for the participants in your group. Ask them to record their responses and then share their stories.

(10 minutes)

What are any disadvantages to our calling God "mother"?

Is it helpful for you to think of Holy Communion as "food of light"? Why or why not?

THE BIBLICAL STORY

Invite participants to find the passages in their Bibles and record responses to the questions.

Mothering God, you gave me birth in the bright morning of this world

In Genesis 1:2, God's spirit breathes over water to create the earth. In Genesis 2:7, God is like a sculptor, forming Adam from clay. Which description do you prefer?

Creator, source of every breath, you are my rain, my wind, my sun

Psalm 147:8, 18 praises God for sending rain and wind, and Christians praise God for creating rain and wind. In what ways is it helpful to describe our creator as actually being rain and wind?

Psalm 1:3 is one of many biblical passages that, like text composer Janzen, uses nature imagery to describe human beings. Human beings are like trees yielding fruit. Are we more like trees, or less like trees? Discuss. What other images come to mind?

Determine if your group would prefer to:

◆ read and respond to all passages and questions before talking

◆ read, respond, and discuss one passage at a time

(20 minutes)

Probably because biblical writers saw their God as very different from the goddesses worshipped by their neighbors, only a few passages in the Bible describe God as a mother. Read and discuss Deuteronomy 32:18, Isaiah 49:15, Hosea 11:1-4, and Matthew 23:37. In your experience, how is God like a nursing mother?

LIVING THE STORY

Invite participants to reflect for a few moments on today's conversation, and then respond to the questions. It is important to share the responses to these questions so your group can offer prayer support to each other throughout the week.

Select a leader for your next meeting and remind everyone of the time and location.

Close by singing "Mothering God, You Gave Me Birth" and praying together.
(10 minutes)

How and where do you anticipate that God will bring anything to birth this week?

How can we mother one another?

Which image of the Creator God in this hymn will stick with you this week? Why?

O God our Creator,
    you are the source of our every breath.
    You rain down your mercy on us,
    and you shine the light of your grace
    throughout the entire earth.
(Silence for private prayer.)
Create us anew each day.
    Form us to be your arms, that we may
    extend your loving care to all creation;
through Jesus Christ,
    our Savior and Lord. Amen

PRAISE AND THANKSGIVING

1 Praise and thanks - giv - ing, Fa - ther, we of - fer for all things
2 Bless, Lord, the la - bor we bring to serve you, that with our
3 Fa - ther, pro - vid - ing food for your chil - dren, by your wise
4 Then will your bless - ing reach ev - 'ry peo - ple, free - ly con -

liv - ing, cre - at - ed good: har - vest of sown fields, fruits of the
neigh-bor we may be fed. Sow - ing or till - ing, we would work
guid - ing teach us to share one with an - oth - er, so that, re -
fess - ing your gra - cious hand. Where all o - bey you, no one will

or - chard, hay from the mown fields, blos - som and wood.
with you, har - vest - ing, mill - ing for dai - ly bread.
joic - ing with us, all oth - ers may know your care.
hun - ger; in your love's sway you nour - ish the land.

GATHERING FOR THE STORY

Greet participants as they arrive. Invite them to record their responses to these questions in their book.

A Bible concordance would be a helpful tool for people who want to list text citations or search for stories by key words.

Begin with introductions. Ask volunteers to share the stories they selected, then say the prayer together.

Invite the group to sing "Praise and Thanksgiving" (see page 23).
(10 minutes)

In our thinking about Thanksgiving Day, we need to be mindful that, for some, this is a day of mourning, not thanksgiving and rejoicing. These stories need to be heard as well.

Describe your Thanksgiving Day traditions. In what ways is thanksgiving to God a part of those traditions?

How is/might worship be a part of the day's activities?

How might every day be one of thanksgiving?

O God, our Lord and Creator,
  we bring you praise and thanksgiving
  for all your plenteous creation.
Your gracious hand offers us food to eat
  and opportunity to share.
Bless us during this hour with
  a time of prayer, a space for learning,
  and a connection with one another;
through Jesus Christ,
  our Savior and Lord. Amen

PRAISE AND THANKSGIVING

Praise and thanksgiving, Father, we offer
for all things living, created good:
harvest of sown fields, fruits of the orchard,
hay from the mown fields, blossom and wood.

Bless, Lord, the labor we bring to serve you,
that with our neighbor we may be fed.
Sowing or tilling, we would work with you,
harvesting, milling for daily bread.

Father, providing food for your children,
by your wise guiding teach us to share
one with another, so that, rejoicing
with us, all others may know your care.

Then will your blessing reach ev'ry people,
freely confessing your gracious hand.
Where all obey you, no one will hunger;
in your love's sway you nourish the land.

LEARNING THE STORY

After participants read the background of this hymn, talk about information they found meaningful or helpful.

(5 minutes)

The text

This hymn was written by Albert F. Bayly (1901–1984) and was first published in 1967. Bayly was a British Congregational parish minister who wrote not only Christian hymns but also the words for three cantatas.

The tune

Bayly wrote this hymn to fit BUNESSAN, a lovely Gaelic tune that he thought was underused. This tune was first published in 1888 by Alexander Fraser, who transcribed the music from a Scottish Highland singer.

The legend

Bayly wrote of this hymn that Christians can thank God rightly for creation only if they are ready to share God's gifts with others. The hymn expresses well the Jewish and Christian practice that at harvest time, the community not only has a grand feast, but also praises God for the food and shares with those who are hungry.

OUR STORY

What does stanza 2 mean for people who do not farm? Explain.

You may need to adapt these questions for the participants in your group. Ask them to record their responses and then share their stories.

(10 minutes)

How do you think God is like a father who provides food for us, God's children?

Granting the diversity of world religions, what does it mean that "every people" will confess God as the creator and provider?

THE BIBLICAL STORY

Invite participants to find the passages in their Bibles and record responses to the questions.

Psalm 65 is one of Scripture's most beautiful Thanksgiving Day poems. In verses 6-8, God creates the world by taming the wild seas. What do you think of this description?

In your love's sway you nourish the land

Verses 9-13 are a poetic description of God nurturing the earth so it can provide us with food. Today's hymn also says that God continually nourishes the land. What evidence could you find to suggest our culture thinks of God as providing us with food?

In verse 1, the worshipper speaks of vows. In gratitude, the believer made promises to God. What are some examples of vows we make to God? Should we make such vows?

By your wise guiding teach us to share one with another

Where does our covenant with God lead us? Why is this important?

Determine if your group would prefer to:

◆ read and respond to all passages and questions before talking

◆ read, respond, and discuss one passage at a time

(20 minutes)

Exodus 23:16, 19 says that the Israelites were expected to offer to the priests the best of the first fruits of the harvest. Leviticus 27:30-32 says that the tithe, ten percent of the harvest, belongs to the Lord. If you come from a tithing tradition, talk about it. Do you think God cares if we tithe? What does Scripture seem to suggest? What does the act of tithing suggest?

LIVING THE STORY

Invite participants to reflect for a few moments on today's conversation, and then respond to the questions. It is important to share the responses to these questions so your group can offer prayer support to each other throughout the week.

Select a leader for your next meeting and remind everyone of the time and location.

Close by singing "Praise and Thanksgiving" and praying together. *(10 minutes)*

How often do you give thanks before meals?

If we believe that a loving God provides food, how are we to think about famine?

How should we respond to hunger in the world?

O God, our Lord and Creator,
>   we bring you our praise and thanksgiving
>   for all your abundant creation.
In this country, there is food aplenty.
We thank you for all the food you provide
>   but are mindful that even here,
>   people go hungry.
(Silence for private prayer).
Give us eyes to see your generous gifts,
>   tongues to praise your creation,
>   and hands to share your bounty;
through Jesus Christ,
>   our Savior and Lord. Amen

GOD, WHO STRETCHED THE SPANGLED HEAVENS

1 God, who stretched the span-gled heav - ens in - fi - nite in time and place,
2 We have ven - tured worlds un - dreamed of since the child-hood of our race;
3 As each far ho - ri - zon beck - ons, may it chal-lenge us a - new:

flung the suns in burn-ing ra - diance through the si - lent fields of space:
known the ec - sta - sy of wing-ing through un - trav-eled realms of space;
chil - dren of cre - a - tive pur - pose, serv - ing oth-ers, hon-'ring you.

we, your chil - dren in your like-ness, share in - ven - tive pow'rs with you;
probed the se - crets of the at - om, yield-ing un - i - mag - ined pow'r,
May our dreams prove rich with prom-ise; each en-deav-or well be - gun;

great Cre - a - tor, still cre - at - ing, show us what we yet may do.
fac - ing us with life's de - struc - tion or our most tri - um-phant hour.
great Cre - a - tor, give us guid-ance till our goals and yours are one.

Text: Catherine Cameron, b. 1927, alt. Words © 1967 by Hope Publishing Co., Carol Stream, IL 60188. All rights reserved.
Music: HOLY MANNA, W. Walker, *Southern Harmony*, 1835. Arr. © 1969 *Contemporary Worship I: Hymns*, admin. Augsburg Fortress.

GATHERING FOR THE STORY

Greet participants as they arrive. Invite them to record their responses to this question in their book.

A Bible concordance would be a helpful tool for people who want to list text citations or search for stories by key words.

Begin with introductions. Ask volunteers to share the stories they selected, then say the prayer together.

Invite the group to sing "God, Who Stretched the Spangled Heavens" (see page 31).
(10 minutes)

Have you ever looked at the sky through a telescope? How did it make you feel?

What has science revealed about God's creation? How does that make you feel?

What do you think of travel to the moon? Would you like to go there yourself someday?

How many years do you think it will be before people take trips to the moon other than for science?

O God, great Creator, your creation is
   beyond our seeing,
      outside our knowing.
Our earth is small, and your universe
   is immense.
Open our minds this hour
   to imagine your vastness.
      Open our hearts to one another,
      and guide us toward your truths;
through Jesus Christ,
   our Savior and Lord. Amen

GOD, WHO STRETCHED THE SPANGLED HEAVENS

God, who stretched the spangled heavens
infinite in time and place,
flung the suns in burning radiance
through the silent fields of space:
we, your children in your likeness,
share inventive pow'rs with you;
great Creator, still creating,
show us what we yet may do.

We have ventured worlds undreamed of
since the childhood of our race;
known the ecstasy of winging
through untraveled realms of space;
probed the secrets of the atom,
yielding unimagined pow'r,
facing us with life's destruction
or our most triumphant hour.

As each far horizon beckons,
may it challenge us anew:
children of creative purpose,
serving others, hon'ring you.
May our dreams prove rich with promise;
each endeavor well begun;
great Creator, give us guidance
till our goals and yours are one.

Catherine Cameron, b. 1927, alt.
Words © 1967 by Hope Publishing Co., Carol Stream, IL 60188. All rights reserved.

LEARNING THE STORY

After participants read the background of this hymn, talk about information they found meaningful or helpful.

(5 minutes)

The text

Catherine Arnott Cameron (b. 1927) lives in California and has taught social psychology on the university level. This hymn was first published in 1969, the same year as the first lunar landing by humans (Apollo 11, July 20, 1969). It was revised for its publication in the Lutheran Book of Worship in 1978.

The tune

The tune HOLY MANNA was composed by William Moore and first appeared in a hymn collection in 1825. The melody line is called *pentatonic*, which means that only five notes of the scale are used: C, D, F, G, and A.

The legend

The author Catherine Cameron said that she wrote this hymn over a period of several months at a time when she was experiencing a new sense of creativity in her own life. With its very contemporary description of the universe, this hymn refers to intangible wonders, such as space and the atom, rather than to flowers and birds, those tangible parts of creation that we encounter daily.

OUR STORY

Describe a time when you felt most creative. What did you create?

You may need to adapt these questions for the participants in your group. Ask them to record their responses and then share their stories.

(10 minutes)

Cite some examples of human creativity that follow the purposes of God.

Are there examples of human creativity opposing God's purposes? Explain.

THE BIBLICAL STORY

Invite participants to find the passages in their Bibles and record responses to the questions.

Flung the suns in burning radiance through the silent fields of space

Even though the writer of Genesis 1 lived at a time when the earth was understood to be the center of creation, Genesis 1:14-18 says that God created the sun, moon, and stars. How might Genesis 1 be useful to us, given our scientific understanding of the universe?

God, who stretched the spangled heavens infinite in time and space

How do we reconcile creation with evolution in our science-oriented world?

We, your children, in your likeness, share inventive pow'rs with you

Genesis 1:26 claims that humans are created in the image of God. What does it mean that all humans are made in God's image?

Determine if your group would prefer to:

◆ read and respond to all passages and questions before talking

◆ read, respond, and discuss one passage at a time

(20 minutes)

Facing us with life's destruction or our most triumphant hour

Genesis 3:5 suggests that trying to be like God is a temptation for sin. Ephesians 4:22-24 says that we are created in the likeness of God to be holy. This hymn suggests that our creative powers make us like God. What are the blessings and dangers of this view? Why?

LIVING THE STORY

Invite participants to reflect for a few moments on today's conversation, and then respond to the questions. It is important to share the responses to these questions so your group can offer prayer support to each other throughout the week.

Select a leader for your next meeting and remind everyone of the time and location.

Close by singing "God, Who Stretched the Spangled Heavens" and praying together.
(10 minutes)

How can we know God's goals?

How do technological advances help you to live a creative Christian life? Explain.

How might technology get in your way?

O God, great Creator,
> your creation stuns us with its power
> and beauty. Your many suns are farther
> than our telescopes can see,
> and the particles in the atom
> are too tiny for our minds.
(Silence for private prayer.)
Give us joy in the immensity of your universe,
> and shape our creativity
> toward your purposes;
through Jesus Christ,
> our Savior and Lord. Amen

IN SACRED MANNER

1 In sa - cred man - ner may we walk up -
2 In sa - cred man - ner may we see the
3 In sa - cred man - ner may we touch the
4 In sa - cred man - ner may we hear the
5 In sa - cred man - ner may we live a -
6 In sa - cred man - ner may we walk up -

on the fair and lov - ing earth, in beau - ty move, in
lu - mi - nous and lov - ing stars, with won - der and with
sus - pir - ant and lov - ing green, give hon - or and give
pound - ing waves, the sear - ing fire, the rush - ing wind, the
mong the wise and lov - ing ones, sit hum - bly, as at
on the fair and lov - ing earth, in beau - ty move, in

beau - ty love the liv - ing round that brought us birth. We
awe be - hold their ev - er - new cre - a - tive pow'rs. The
grat - i - tude for shade, for bloom, for gift un - seen. The
sing - ing night, the for - est hymn, the lov - ing choir. The
sa - ges' feet, by four - legged, finned and feath - ered ones. The
beau - ty love the liv - ing round that brought us birth. We

stand on ho - ly ground. We stand on ho - ly ground.
heav - ens show us God. The heav - ens show us God.
trees shall shout for joy. The trees shall shout for joy.
morn - ing stars shall sing. The morn - ing stars shall sing.
an - i - mals will teach. The an - i - mals will teach.
stand on ho - ly ground. We stand on ho - ly ground.

Text © 1990 Susan Palo Cherwin, admin. Augsburg Fortress.
Music: SEATTLE, Robert Buckley Farlee. © 1997 Augsburg Fortress.

GATHERING FOR THE STORY

Greet participants as they arrive. Invite them to record their responses to this question in their book.

A Bible concordance would be a helpful tool for people who want to list text citations or search for stories by key words.

Begin with introductions. Ask volunteers to share the stories they selected, then say the prayer together.

Invite the group to sing "In Sacred Manner" (see page 39).
(10 minutes)

Some Native American religions hold the created order in high esteem. Most Christians have only recently rediscovered this piece of their tradition. Describe how in your life you revere the creation. Describe how your faith community might revere the creation.

Describe a time when it might be appropriate to use drums in church.

O God, holy One, O God, mighty One,
  we meet together on the holy ground
  that your power and mercy
  have created. The earth brings us
  your love.
Visit us this hour with your power
  and your mercy. Show us your earth,
  show us your word,
  and show us one another;
through Jesus Christ,
  our Savior and Lord. Amen

IN SACRED MANNER

In sacred manner may we walk upon the fair and loving earth,
in beauty move, in beauty love the living round that brought us birth.
We stand on holy ground. We stand on holy ground.

In sacred manner may we see the luminous and loving stars,
with wonder and with awe behold their ever-new creative powers.
The heavens show us God. The heavens show us God.

In sacred manner may we touch the suspirant and loving green,
give honor and give gratitude for shade, for bloom, for gift unseen.
The trees shall shout for joy. The trees shall shout for joy.

In sacred manner may we hear the pounding waves, the searing fire,
the rushing wind, the singing night, the forest hymn, the loving choir.
The morning stars shall sing. The morning stars shall sing.

In sacred manner may we live among the wise and loving ones,
sit humbly, as at sages' feet, by four-legged, finned, and feathered ones.
The animals will teach. The animals will teach.

In sacred manner may we walk upon the fair and loving earth,
in beauty move, in beauty love the living round that brought us birth.
We stand on holy ground. We stand on holy ground.

LEARNING THE STORY

Invite a participant to accompany the hymn singing with a small drum.

After participants read the hymn background, talk about information they found meaningful or helpful.

(5 minutes)

The text

Susan Palo Cherwien (b. 1953) is a Lutheran musician, poet, and hymnwriter who lives in Minnesota. She first published this hymn in 1995.

The tune

Robert Buckley Farlee (b. 1950) is a Lutheran church musician, composer, and pastor. He has composed the music for several of Cherwien's hymn texts. The tune is named SEATTLE after the renowned Native American Christian chief of the Suquamish tribe.

The legend

Cherwien reports that she wrote this hymn in response to a course she took focusing on the fate of the earth. Each stanza begins with the Native American prayer that we walk on the earth in a sacred manner.

OUR STORY

What does it mean to walk "in sacred manner"?

You may need to adapt these questions for the participants in your group. Ask them to record their responses and then share their stories.
(10 minutes)

What would it mean for Christians to call the earth "holy ground"?

Is a church building more holy than a city park?

Describe a time when an animal taught you.

THE BIBLICAL STORY

Invite participants to find the passages in their Bibles and record responses to the questions.

We stand on holy ground

Stanza 1 quotes Exodus 3:5. God tells Moses to remove his shoes, since he is standing on holy ground. What makes the earth holy?

The heavens show us God

Stanza 2 recalls Psalm 19:1, saying that the heavens declare God's glory. What can the sky teach us about God? What can and do we learn from nature?

The trees shall shout for joy

Stanza 3 cites Psalm 96:12, where the trees are shouting for joy. Many Christians sing this psalm on Christmas Eve. In stanza 4, "the morning stars sing" quotes Job 38:7, part of another biblical description of how God created the world. How does this kind of poetry speak to you?

Determine if your group would prefer to:
◆ read and respond to all passages and questions before talking
◆ read, respond, and discuss one passage at a time

(20 minutes)

The animals will teach

Stanza 5 quotes Job 12:7, which says that the animals will teach us about God's wisdom and power. The Christian church has never said much about our learning from animals. What would be the benefit of such conversation?

LIVING THE STORY

Invite participants to reflect for a few moments on today's conversation, and then respond to the questions. It is important to share the responses to these questions so your group can offer prayer support to each other throughout the week.

Since this is the last session, take a few minutes to talk about future study this group might want to pursue.

Close by singing "In Sacred Manner," or you may wish to sing all five hymns from *Hymns to the Creator*. End the session by praying together.
(10 minutes)

How might Christians learn about ecology from other world religions?

How might you do sacred walking this week?

O God, holy One, O God, mighty One,
    together with the trees and the animals,
    we live on your holy ground.
(Silence for private prayer.)
Show us your love dwelling inside
    your creation. Join us with all the elders
    and sages of time past to praise your love
    and honor your earth;
through Jesus Christ,
    our Savior and Lord. Amen

RESOURCES

Your church's music director, the public library, or the Internet may be good places to start looking for recordings of the hymns discussed in this volume.